SELF-CARE
FIRST-AID KIT

SELF-CARE FIRST-AID KIT

Copyright © Octopus Publishing Group Limited, 2026

All rights reserved.

Text by Jayne Hardy

No part of this book may be reproduced by any means, nor transmitted, nor translated into a machine language, without the written permission of the publishers.

Condition of Sale
This book is sold subject to the condition that it shall not, by way of trade or otherwise, be lent, resold, hired out or otherwise circulated in any form of binding or cover other than that in which it is published and without a similar condition including this condition being imposed on the subsequent purchaser.

An Hachette UK Company
www.hachette.co.uk

Vie Books, an imprint of Summersdale Publishers
Part of Octopus Publishing Group Limited
Carmelite House
50 Victoria Embankment
LONDON
EC4Y 0DZ
UK

This FSC® label means that materials and other controlled sources used for the product have been responsibly sourced

www.summersdale.com

The authorized representative in the EEA is Hachette Ireland, 8 Castlecourt Centre, Dublin 15, D15 XTP3, Ireland (email: info@hbgi.ie)

Printed and bound in China

ISBN: 978-1-83799-751-0
eISBN: 978-1-83799-752-7

Substantial discounts on bulk quantities of Summersdale books are available to corporations, professional associations and other organizations. For details contact general enquiries: telephone: +44 (0) 1243 771107 or email: enquiries@summersdale.com.

SELF-CARE
FIRST-AID KIT

Tips and Techniques to Help You Practise
Self-Care for Mind, Body and Spirit

ANNA BARNES

Disclaimer

Neither the author nor the publisher can be held responsible for any injury, loss or claim – be it health, financial or otherwise – arising out of the use, or misuse, of the suggestions made herein. This book is not intended as a substitute for the medical advice of a doctor or physician. If you are experiencing problems with your physical or mental health, it is always best to follow the advice of a medical professional.

CONTENTS

Introduction	6
How to Use This Book	8
Chapter One: Self-Care 101	10
Chapter Two: Body	46
Chapter Three: Mind	82
Chapter Four: Spirit	118
Conclusion	152
Resources	154
Index	155

INTRODUCTION

This book was made for "those days"... You know, the ones when everything feels a bit too much, when you're running on empty, and when even asking yourself what you need feels like one question too many.

It's for the moments when you can't quite catch your breath, or your thoughts, or your usual way of coping. The moments when you feel as though you should know what would help, but your brain is foggy, your body is tired, and your heart feels like it's somewhere off in the distance.

This is a book full of tiny self-care lifelines. Some soothing, some gently energizing. Some practical, some playful. They're here to hold you up, inch you forward or simply help you stay where you are, safely, until the fog begins to lift.

You won't find strict routines, unrealistic goals or overwhelming advice here. Instead, you'll find soft ideas for caring for your body, mind and spirit. These are ideas you can dip into and try in your own way, at your own pace. You don't need to start at the beginning. You don't need to try everything. This is a book that's meant to meet you where you are.

Whatever brings you here, and however you're feeling, know this: there is no wrong way to take care of yourself. There is no shame in needing support. And there is nothing selfish about learning to meet your needs. In fact, this is something we'd all benefit from, one way or another.

You are worthy of that care – not later, not when you've done enough, but now. Especially now.

So come as you are. This book is here to help you gather the most helpful tools. Not to fix yourself – but to be with yourself, kindly, through it all.

HOW TO USE THIS BOOK

There's no one right way to use this book. There's no reading order, no rigid plan and no expectation that you'll try every single thing. Think of this as your self-care toolkit – here when you need it, quiet when you don't, easy to dip into in the moments you feel a bit frayed around the edges.

Some days, you might be looking for something soothing. Other days, you might be running on empty and just need a quick spark of something – anything – that helps you feel more okay. Let your energy lead the way. You can flick through and land on a page at random, follow a theme, or mark pages to return to when life wobbles.

You'll notice the book is arranged into themes: care for the body, mind and spirit. But every tool you find here has the potential to soothe you in more ways than one. A walk might clear your head and boost your mood. A bubble bath might settle your body and help you press pause. Self-care doesn't live in neat little boxes and neither do you.

You might want to keep a pen or Post-it notes nearby, or even create your own self-care toolkit as you go. You can write in the margins, dog-ear the pages and tuck the book under your pillow. Let it be yours; let it feel lived in.

Most of all, use this book with kindness. Do not use it as a stick to beat yourself with but rather as a quiet reminder that no matter how you're feeling, you are worth caring for.

However you're showing up today, this book is here for support in whatever way you need it.

CHAPTER ONE:
SELF-CARE 101

Self-care gets talked about a lot, so it's easy to lose sight of what it *really* means. Despite the hashtags and viral videos, it's not all bubble baths, expensive beauty products and spa days. At its core, self-care is about meeting our individual needs with care and attention. It's the stuff that helps us function, recover and keep going, *even* when life is hard (especially when life is hard).

This chapter lays the foundations. What self-care is and what it isn't, the common obstacles we face and how to overcome those, how to spot when we need more of it and how to make it work in real life, with all its ups, downs and busyness.

We'll keep things simple, helpful and doable. No overwhelm, no pressure, just a starting point toward helping us care for ourselves in ways that work.

WHAT IS SELF-CARE?

Self-care is the act of tending to your body, mind and spirit in ways that feel supportive and sustaining, benefiting your overall health and resilience. It's the little check-ins and the big pivots. The soft blankets and the firm boundaries. The deep breaths and the dance breaks. It's anything that helps you feel more you – grounding you and helping you feel better able to face whatever life brings.

Self-care is for everyone. It's not reserved for people with spare time, spare cash or a curated shelf of fancy candles. It's for all of us messy, magnificent, muddling-through humans. Your self-care doesn't need to look like anyone else's. It only needs to feel like care.

It's not always pretty. Sometimes, it's flossing your teeth or making that appointment. Other times, it's letting yourself cry, say *no* or nap at noon.

Self-care is not to be dismissed for, at its heart, it is incredibly functional. When cared for, we cope better with stress, bounce back quicker after hard days and show up more fully for ourselves and others.

WHY SELF-CARE MATTERS

We can't pour from an empty cup, and we're not meant to run on fumes. You see, the body always keeps score. Stress, burnout, grief – those feelings and emotions don't just live in our heads. The toll appears on our shoulders, in how we sleep, on our skin and in how we view the world. And, left unaddressed, that toll only grows heavier.

Self-care ripples outward and affects every aspect of our lives. When we're cared for, we feel differently and we show up differently; for work, for relationships, for the world, *for ourselves*. Self-care isn't selfish: it's the scaffolding which holds us up and helps us function, recover and connect.

Self-care is also a form of self-respect. When we care for ourselves, we say: I am worth the effort. I am deserving. I am worthy. I matter. And that changes *everything*.

THE THREE MAIN TYPES OF SELF-CARE

Self-care comes in many shapes and forms, but it tends to fall into three main buckets: physical, mental, and emotional/spiritual. These aren't separate silos; they constantly and intrinsically overlap and influence one another.

Physical self-care

This is anything that helps us take care of our body. That might mean getting enough sleep, drinking water, taking medication, walking or feeding ourselves something nourishing. It can also mean moving our body in a way that feels good or lying still with a hot water bottle when that's what's needed. It's not about pushing through; it's about responding to what our body needs with care.

Mental self-care

Mental self-care is about taking care of our mind. That might mean creating space for rest, learning, focus or release. It can look like journalling, reading

something that expands our thinking, taking a break from screens, doing a puzzle or speaking our thoughts aloud to a trusted friend.

Emotional and spiritual self-care

This is all about our inner world, our essence, the part of us that seeks connection, meaning, peace, purpose and comfort. Emotional and spiritual self-care might involve therapy, meditation, prayer, lighting a candle, spending time in nature, listening to music that resonates or creating something just for the joy of it. It helps us feel grounded, soothed and realigned.

Remember: what supports one part of us often supports the other parts, too.

SELF-CARE IS ABOUT PRESENCE

Self-care isn't just reserved for the big, visible acts and neither do we have to wait for the "perfect" self-care moment. The tiny stuff counts and compounds. In fact, self-care is less about what it looks like and more about what it feels like.

If it helps us feel supported, soothed, resourced, nourished, held or steadied, then it's self-care. If it stops the spiral or starts to replenish our energy, it is also self-care. If it brings us home to ourselves, even just a little – yup, that's self-care, too.

The thing about self-care is that it never has to be impressive, seen or shared. When we set off with that intention of making it look a certain way, we dilute its power. Self-care isn't at all about performance, but rather presence: how can we carefully and kindly tend to ourselves right now?

SELF-CARE LOOKS DIFFERENT FOR EVERYONE

It's easy to feel like we're doing self-care "wrong" when we compare it to someone else's. But your version doesn't have to look like anyone else's. It only has to feel like care *to you*.

What soothes one person might irritate another. What energizes someone else might leave you exhausted. Some people run marathons for self-care. Others need to sit quietly in their dressing gown and stare into space. What's right for you will change and evolve as you do.

The key is tuning in, not copying out. Notice what helps you exhale. What lifts your shoulders a little. What makes you feel more like you. That's *your* kind of care.

Comparison will only lead you away from yourself. Intuition will lead you home. Your self-care doesn't need to be pretty, shareable or impressive. It just needs to work – for you.

THE SIGNS WE NEED MORE SELF-CARE

Sometimes, it builds slowly. We carry on as usual, thinking we're managing just fine until, suddenly, the tiniest things feel impossible. Often, the signs were there long before the overwhelm hit. They were in the quiet nudges and the gentle warnings – all asking for a little more care. Nudges and gentle warnings that are so easy to ignore in a world which conditions us to keep on keeping on.

Physical signs

The body typically speaks first (minds take a while to catch up). We might notice our sleep disruption, trouble falling asleep, waking too early or not feeling rested. Our limbs may feel heavy, and our movements slower. Headaches creep in, our shoulders tighten and digestion goes off course. These are signs that something is out of balance.

Mental signs

We beat ourselves up for lacking in some way when we notice our concentration has slipped or thoughts are running away with themselves. There's a treacly fog that has settled in. But it's not that we're broken: we're depleted and have usually been carrying too much for too long.

Emotional signs

The emotional clues that more self-care is needed are when they start to feel as though they're "all or nothing". All the feels, quick tears, irritability, dread, doom and gloom are signs that something is awry, as is a persistent indifference, apathy and a loss of interest in the outcome of a situation.

Behavioural signs

We stop doing the things that usually help. We retreat. We let small tasks pile up because thinking about them feels too much. We scroll more. Avoid more. Drift more. That's exhaustion in disguise.

WHAT SELF-CARE ISN'T

It's easy to get the wrong idea about self-care – especially when it's filtered through social media or packaged as something shiny and perfect. But real self-care? It's much gentler, messier and more human than that.

- + Self-care isn't about performing a version of wellness or ticking things off a checklist.
- + It's not reserved for people who already have everything else under control.
- + It isn't always glamorous or fun.
- + It's not a fix-all.
- + It won't erase our stress overnight or solve every problem we face.
- + It's not one-size-fits-all.
- + It's not a luxury.
- + It's not something we have to earn.
- + And it's *definitely* not selfish.

Self-care is simply how we take care of ourselves, bit by bit, especially when things feel hard. It's a practice, not a performance.

SELF-CARE ON A BUDGET

Self-care doesn't have to cost anything. It's not defined by spa days, luxury skincare or pricey subscriptions. Some of the most powerful self-care tools are free: sunlight, water, silence, sleep, movement and boundaries.

Marketing has muddied the message. But at its core, self-care is about tending to your needs in whatever way is available to you. This might be sitting with a cup of tea, standing barefoot on the grass, swapping a doomscroll for a walk and talking kindly to yourself.

When the budget is tight, focus on what brings comfort, clarity, connection or calm. It could be a library book, a nap, a handwritten note to your future self or a long soak in the tub.

Self-care doesn't live in your bank account. It lives in your choices. And the smallest ones can hold the most power.

MAKING TIME FOR SELF-CARE

It's easy to tell ourselves there's no time. Let's face it: life is loud, and there's never a shortage of things vying for our attention. Self-care all too easily slips to the bottom of the list (if it ever made it onto the list in the first place).

One of the biggest misconceptions about self-care is that a big chunk of time is needed. In reality, it often exists in the in-between bits. Going for a walk on our lunch break. Standing still for 5 minutes while the kettle boils. Taking a break before responding to that message that's triggered something inside of us.

Another misconception is that we have no time, when how we spend our time is negotiable. We can free up more of it when we notice where it's leaking. How long do we scroll before bed? How often do we say *yes* when we mean *no*? Are there things we're doing out of habit or fear of letting someone down? How often do we take on too much simply because we didn't ask for help when we could have or were afraid to say *no*?

Self-care doesn't need to be another task. It's what helps us carry all the others. It's the base layer. The bit that steadies us when everything else feels unsteady.

Small shifts matter. A glass of water on your desk. Five minutes of quiet before the day begins. A gentler bedtime. A pause before reacting. A firmer boundary around what drains you.

Think of self-care as intentional anchors woven into the day, reminding us that we matter and our needs are important.

Our greatest glory is not in never falling, but in rising every time we fall.

CONFUCIUS

SELF-CARE AND WORTHINESS

This is the quiet core of it all: do we believe we deserve to feel well and happy? Do we believe we're worthy of rest, care and the same compassion we offer to others?

So many of us carry a deep, old story that says we must earn care. By being good. By being productive. By being selfless. And indeed, the messaging around us reinforces this again and again.

But we're all worthy of care simply because we exist. Not when we've ticked enough boxes. Not when we've given enough. *Now*.

When we begin to believe we're worthy of care, everything changes. We start choosing differently. Speaking kindlier to ourselves. Listening to our needs instead of overriding them.

Worthiness isn't something we wait for. It's something we practise. Self-care is not a reward for being perfect. It's a tool which helps us make the best of our days.

SELF-CARE WHEN WE'RE ALREADY DEPLETED AND LOW ON ENERGY

When we're at our lowest, doing anything, let alone self-care, feels impossible. The idea of adding anything like another task or another expectation feels like the final straw. But this is when we need it most. Not the polished, aspirational kind. The quiet, survival kind that acknowledges exactly where we're at.

This is where the Spoon Theory can be of help. Originally created within disabled and chronic illness communities, it offers a way to describe and honour limited energy. It suggests that we each start the day with a certain number of "spoons", a metaphor for our energy. Everything we do takes a spoon. Made the bed? Used a spoon. Taken a shower? Used a spoon. Pondered over a decision? Yup, used a spoon. Attended a work meeting? Used a spoon, or three…

Some days, we start the day with more spoons than on others. A rough night's sleep would deplete our

spoons, whereas a good night's sleep would replenish them. There are tough days which force us to borrow spoons from the coming day, leaving us short when that day arrives. On days when spoons are scarce, self-care isn't about thriving but preservation.

When we've got nothing left to give, self-care is about getting through. Focusing on the next hour, not the next day. What needs attention right now? What can wait?

Self-care here might be brushing your teeth while sitting down. It might be asking someone else to help. It might be choosing toast over nothing.

Low-energy self-care isn't lesser. It's the vital sort, the tender art of still showing up for yourself, even when you feel like you've got nothing left to give.

WE DON'T HAVE TO EARN REST

Rest isn't something we only deserve once we've ticked everything off. It's not a reward for pushing through. It's a basic need – like food, water or air.

Still, many of us resist it. We fill every gap in the day. We feel guilty for sitting down. We tell ourselves we'll rest *later* once we've done a bit more. But later rarely comes; in the meantime, we run on fumes.

Rest isn't laziness. It's how we recover, how we come back to ourselves. Sometimes, it looks like sleep. Other times, it's stepping away from noise, saying *no* or letting something wait. It might be staring out the window, moving slowly, laughing or doing nothing.

We don't need permission to rest. We don't have to explain it. We just have to notice when we're running low or need a break and let that be reason enough.

BOUNDARIES ARE SELF-CARE

Boundaries aren't walls. They're more like doors with handles on *your* side. They help you decide what comes in, what stays out, and what's simply too much right now. They're how we protect our time, energy and well-being. And yes, they can feel uncomfortable, especially if we've spent years putting others first.

But when we live without boundaries, something slowly drains. We say *yes* when we mean *no*. We keep giving, even when we're already stretched too thin. We quiet our own needs to avoid disappointing others.

Setting a boundary can be simple, but that doesn't mean it's easy. It might look like pausing before replying to an email or message. Turning off notifications. Saying, "I can't this week." Logging off when our brain feels loud. Taking a breath before committing.

Boundaries aren't selfish. They're a way of making space for all that matters to us. Every boundary we set is a way of saying: I count too.

HOW TO IDENTIFY OUR SELF-CARE NEEDS

Some days, we feel scattered and need something to bring us back to earth. On other days, we feel flat and need a little lift. There are times we long for company and times we want quiet. Our needs aren't fixed – they shift with our energy, emotions, environment and season of life.

Start with curiosity

A gentle check-in can go a long way. Ask yourself, *How am I, really?* Not just emotionally but physically, mentally and energetically. Am I tense? Restless? Flat? Overstimulated? Worn thin? Self-care begins when we notice what's happening beneath the surface. When we meet ourselves exactly as we are, self-care becomes something we *can* do.

Use simple tools to check-in

Some days, words come easily. On others, it helps to have tools. Try a short journalling check-in, record a voice note or do a 2-minute body scan from head to toe. Ask yourself questions like: *What's draining me today? What might help me feel steadier?* You might be surprised by what surfaces when you pause long enough to ask.

Look for the whispers

Our needs don't always speak in complete sentences. They show up in fatigue, forgetfulness, snapping at people we love or zoning out when we're usually tuned in. A headache might be asking for water. Irritability might be asking for rest. Tuning in is how we learn the language of our own care.

There's no "right" answer

There's no perfect formula or single "right" answer. Some days, what helps will surprise us. On other days, nothing works, and that's information, too. The point is to stay in relationship with ourselves. Self-care begins with listening; the more often we tune in, the more we'll hear.

SUPPORT SYSTEMS AS SELF-CARE

We're not meant to do life alone. And yet, asking for help makes us feel vulnerable and like a failure. But reaching out isn't weakness. In fact, it's quite the opposite – it's wisdom.

Support can take on many different guises: a friend who checks in, a neighbour who waves, a therapist who holds space, an online group, a book club. Sometimes, it's someone who listens without jumping in to fix things. Sometimes, it's someone who says, "Have you eaten?" when we've forgotten to notice our own hunger.

We all need reminding, now and then, that we're not carrying it all alone. Letting people in doesn't make us a burden: it makes us human.

It's okay to ask. It's okay to receive. It's okay to lean. Having a support system means knowing who's in our corner and letting them show up when it counts. That, too, is self-care.

SELF-CARE WHEN WE'RE BURNT OUT

When everything feels like too much, even the most minor task can feel impossible. Burnout isn't just tiredness. It's emotional, physical and mental depletion. If that's where you are, pause.

+ Right now is not the time to push through.
+ Strip things back to your bare minimum.
+ Eat something.
+ Cancel the thing.
+ Say *no*.
+ Rest in whatever way is available to you.

What matters is not trying to fix everything but finding one tiny thing that offers relief.

Recovery won't happen in one day, but small acts of self-care add up. Bit by bit, you'll feel more like yourself. Treat yourself the way you'd treat someone you love who's carried on so long without a break.

SELF-CARE WHEN WE FEEL OVERSTIMULATED

Some days, it's all just too much. Too loud. Too bright. Too many tabs open, literally and mentally. Our senses hit capacity, and the urge to shut down creeps in.

When overstimulated, we don't need to do more: we need to do less. We can:

+ Start by reducing sensory input.
+ Turn off the music.
+ Dim the lights.
+ Close a few tabs.
+ Step away from your phone.
+ Choose quiet over noise, soft over sharp, and slow over fast.
+ Give your system a chance to settle.
+ If you can, sit somewhere still.
+ Breathe in and out through your nose slowly.

Overstimulation isn't you being dramatic; it's your nervous system waving a little flag, asking for less. Let your self-care be subtraction, not addition. Less talking, less deciding, less doing.

PAUSE, REST, RETURN HOME TO YOURSELF

SELF-CARE WHEN WE CAN'T GET A MOMENT ALONE

There are seasons where solitude just isn't available. We're surrounded by noise, needs and people who love us and still leave us stretched thin.

It's hard to hear ourselves think, let alone rest. When space is scarce, we look for pockets. Such as:

+ Pausing while the kettle boils.
+ Taking longer in the bathroom.
+ Standing still and stretching before loading the washing machine.
+ Putting in headphones without playing anything.
+ Whispering and repeating something kind in our minds.
+ Arranging a reprieve to look forward to.

Self-care doesn't always look like an hour alone in a calm room. Sometimes, it's finding a quiet thread to grasp and holding on to it tight.

SELF-CARE WHEN OUR MENTAL HEALTH FLARES

When our mental health dips, it can feel like everything is more challenging. Our thoughts might race or loop. We might feel flat, foggy, heavy or brittle. The smallest things can take the most energy.

In these moments, we need care that meets us where we are and not where we think we *should* be. We can:

+ Lower the bar.
+ Renegotiate expectations.
+ Ease up on what you're asking of yourself.
+ Tell someone safe what's going on.
+ Realize tiny wins are enough.
+ Remember that the world is lucky to have you in it.

If all you've done is breathe and survive today, that's enough. Self-care can simply be acknowledging that and seeing it as a win and not a fail.

These moments don't last forever. But while they're here, treat yourself with the same tenderness you'd offer someone you love.

SELF-CARE WHEN WE'RE GRIEVING

Grief is heavy. It alters everything: how we think, feel and move through the day. Some days, it hollows us out, and other days, it catches us off guard. There's no right way to grieve and no clear timeline.

Self-care while grieving is about getting through it and keeping things soft, simple and slow:

+ Let the tears come when they need to.
+ Eat what we can manage.
+ Wrap ourselves in something that brings comfort.
+ Avoid the things that feel like too much.
+ Speak their name.

Grief comes in waves, loud or quiet, sharp or dull. Whatever shape it takes, we move gently, and we rest often.

Self-care won't erase the grief (nor would we want it to), but it helps us carry the weight of the love that's still here, even in the loss.

SELF-CARE WHEN WE'RE IN PAIN

Pain demands our attention and is impossible to ignore. Whether sharp or aching, constant or unpredictable, it can take over the day and strip away our sense of ease.

Even thinking clearly can feel difficult when our body asks so loudly to be noticed.

In these moments, self-care means creating comfort where we can. This looks like:

+ Keeping the things that soothe us close at hand.
+ Choosing clothes that don't press or pinch.
+ Cancelling what doesn't need to happen.
+ Distracting ourselves gently with sound, stories, or light movement.
+ Letting someone know we're hurting.
+ Giving ourselves permission to do less.

Pain can be lonely. It separates us from how we usually feel, move or cope. Self-care here means remembering that we are still whole and still worthy, even when our body is asking more from us than usual.

SELF-CARE WHEN OUR ROUTINE'S BEEN KNOCKED SIDEWAYS

When life changes, it can throw everything off course. Our routine gets blown apart, the days blur and even simple tasks feel unfamiliar.

Until we find our feet again, we might feel unsettled, disoriented, behind or like we've lost our way completely.

This isn't the time to rebuild everything. It's about steadying ourselves in small, workable ways:

+ Do one thing at the same time each day.

+ Set a couple of reminders to give the day some shape.

+ Batch the boring stuff to clear a bit of space.

+ Write down what actually matters today and let the rest wait.

Routines don't have to look like they used to. They just need to support us in this moment, however imperfectly.

SELF-CARE WHEN WE FEEL WE'RE TOO MUCH

Sometimes, it's not just the feelings themselves but the fear that we are too much. Too intense, too emotional, too sensitive. We've heard it in words or felt it in silence. We start to believe we need to shrink ourselves to be easier to love, understand and be around.

But we don't. There's nothing wrong with feeling deeply or being someone so full of life. Try:

+ Naming what's coming up without judging it.
+ Letting it move (crying, writing, shaking, walking).
+ Spending time with someone who doesn't ask you to be less.
+ Turning down the noise that makes you feel like you're wrong.
+ Letting yourself take up space. All of you. Just as you are.

Self-care here means creating space to feel and be without apology.

SELF-CARE WHEN WE FEEL WE'RE NOT ENOUGH

Some days, we carry the weight of not-enoughness – not capable enough, not calm enough, not smart enough, not outgoing enough, not doing as well as we should be. It can settle in slowly or hit all at once, and when it does, it can cloud everything.

Self-care here is about stepping out of that story, even briefly. We can:

+ Speak to ourselves like we would someone we love.
+ Notice what we've managed today, no matter how small.
+ Do something that reminds us we're capable.
+ Take one thing off our plate without guilt.

This feeling might stick around for a bit, but it isn't the truth. The truth is, we are already enough.

SELF-CARE WHEN WE'RE ANGRY AND DON'T KNOW WHY

Anger can rise without warning, seemingly out of nowhere. It hums beneath the surface or flares up unexpectedly. We snap, shut down or feel it fizzing under our skin with no place to go. And we're left wondering, what is this really about?

Self-care here isn't about pushing anger away but giving it a healthy release. We can:

+ Move our bodies to release the tension.

+ Scribble, stomp, shake or speak it out loud.

+ Do something with our hands – wash up, sweep, knit, dig.

+ Name what's underneath it.

Anger often has something important to say. Maybe we're tired. Perhaps something feels unfair. Maybe we've been swallowing too much for too long.

Self-care here is about acknowledging what's real without shame. It's about letting the fire move through without burning us up.

YOU DON'T NEED PERMISSION

You don't need permission to take care of yourself. You never did. But if today feels heavy or you've forgotten what you're allowed to let go of, here are some gentle tips. Take what you need.

+ It's okay to rest before you're exhausted.
+ It's okay to change your mind.
+ It's okay to cancel plans.
+ It's okay to take up space.
+ It's okay to not reply right away.
+ It's okay to say *no*, even if you said *yes* before.
+ It's okay to leave the washing up.
+ It's okay to ask for help.
+ It's okay to feel things deeply.
+ It's okay to need quiet.
+ It's okay to do something just because it brings you joy.
+ It's okay to stop trying for a bit.
+ It's okay to take care of yourself first.
+ It's okay to not be okay.

A GENTLE REMINDER

It's a given that every life will encounter problems and obstacles from time to time. Sometimes, these come thick and fast. Other times, they come big and bold.

This is a reminder, more than anything, that there's nothing you can't and won't overcome; there's nothing that's bigger and bolder than you. But getting through it isn't about pushing forward – it's about caring for ourselves along the way.

Whether you need to batten down the hatches, call in the cavalry, crawl ahead, get scrappy or take time to refortify before you make any move, self-care is a vital part of the process.

On the other side of the obstacle are some of your best days and funniest moments – even if that feels impossible to imagine right now.

CHAPTER TWO:

BODY

Our bodies carry us through tired mornings, long days and tough seasons. They speak in tension, tightness, gut feelings and goosebumps. They remember things we've forgotten. And they keep going, often without thanks or fanfare.

Self-care for the body isn't about changing it. It's about listening to it. Tuning in. Responding with care. That might mean moving, resting, fuelling, softening, stretching, hydrating. It might mean checking in rather than checking out.

This chapter is about offering our bodies the same kindness we're learning to offer our minds and spirits. It's about making space for comfort. Noticing what helps and doing a little more of that. It's about treating ourselves with the care we need to keep showing up in a body that deserves to be cared for, just as it is.

GET THE RIGHT REST

Rest isn't something we have to earn. It's not a luxury or a sign of weakness. It's a basic human need that's just as important as eating, drinking and moving.

There are at least seven types of rest we might need, and self-care means recognizing which one we're missing:

Physical rest is the one we usually think of. Sleep, naps or just lying down. But it can also be stretching out, going for a slow walk or giving tired muscles a break.

Mental rest is a breather from thinking, planning or trying to solve everything. It could be staring out the window, daydreaming or doing something familiar without needing to concentrate.

Sensory rest means stepping away from bright lights, noise, scrolling and notifications. Sometimes we just need silence and soft light.

Emotional rest is space to stop pretending we're fine. It's having a cry, letting ourselves feel something or being honest with someone we trust.

Social rest means time alone, away from conversation – even the good kind. It's permission to be quiet.

Creative rest is about soaking things up instead of creating. Listening to music, noticing colour, absorbing the beauty around us without having to respond.

Spiritual rest is reconnecting to something bigger than us. That might be nature, stillness, prayer or simply remembering what really matters.

The question isn't whether we deserve rest – it's what kind we need most right now.

DRINK SOME WATER

When life gets busy, the basics can often fall by the wayside. Being mildly dehydrated can affect us in various ways, from our energy and focus to our mood and memory. Fatigue, irritability and a foggy head can creep in, and we might experience a dull headache. Sometimes, what we need isn't another coffee or a pep talk – it's a glass of water.

We can keep a bottle nearby, fill our favourite glass, or add lemon, cucumber or berries if it helps us drink more. Hydration is a quiet hero. This is practical, fuss-free everyday self-care. The kind that keeps us going.

Our bodies constantly work to keep us upright, alert and functioning. Drinking water is one small, powerful way we support them in return.

GO FOR A WALK

Walking is one of the simplest ways to care for the body. It supports cardiovascular health, improves circulation, helps regulate blood sugar levels, lowers stress hormones, boosts endorphins and helps calm an overstimulated nervous system. It also aids digestion, supports joint mobility, improves sleep quality and eases tension in the body after long periods of sitting.

The best thing about walking is it can be done anywhere. A walk to the shops, around the block, to and from work or through a nearby park. Even a short walk can help clear tension, lower stress hormones, blow away the cobwebs and settle a busy mind. Stepping outside creates space away from screens, noise and demands. It gets us breathing differently, thinking differently, moving differently and feeling more capable overall. Every step counts.

STAND OUTSIDE BAREFOOT

Taking off our shoes and letting the soles of our feet meet the earth is one of the quickest ways to feel present. We're so often in our heads, spinning through to-do lists, replaying conversations and planning three steps ahead. But standing barefoot in the grass pulls us out of that spin and brings us back to the now.

There's science behind it, too. Grounding (or earthing as it's sometimes known) refers to direct contact with the earth's surface. Research suggests it can reduce inflammation, lower cortisol levels and calm the nervous system. Our bodies carry an electrical charge, and when we make contact with the ground, we absorb free electrons that help neutralize the stress in our systems. In short, it helps us settle.

Self-care can be that uncomplicated: shoes off, feet down and breathe... Here are a few ways we can connect directly with the earth:

+ Kick your shoes off and stand on some grass.
+ Get your hands in the soil. Plant something, pull up weeds or just have a rummage.
+ Sit directly on the ground with legs stretched out.
+ Walk barefoot on the beach.
+ Lean against a tree and let it take your weight.
+ Paddle in a stream.

SHAKE IT OUT

Tension builds up and gets stored in our bodies, and we hold a lot without meaning to – those tense shoulders, the taut jaw, tight back, and hips that feel like they haven't moved in years.

One of the best ways to release the tension is not to be still but to shake. Animals do it all the time. After a stressful event, many mammals shake their bodies to discharge excess adrenaline and bring their nervous systems back into balance.

Our bodies hold on to stress in the same way, and movement helps us release it. We might not do it instinctively, but we can do it deliberately by letting our limbs slack and shaking our bodies from side to side and up and down.

Self-care doesn't always look calm. Sometimes, it looks like a ginormous, full-bodied shake.

STRETCH

Our bodies weren't designed to be hunched and folded for hours on end. And yet, that's where we often find ourselves: curved over screens, crunched into chairs, forgetting that we even have a spine.

Stretching is a simple way to say, enough. It's a recalibration. A roll of the shoulders. A twist at the waist. A lean to the side that makes everything go click. We don't need a yoga mat or a perfect technique. We just need a willingness to move differently for a minute or two.

Start with where it feels tight. Follow the tension. Reach, rotate, breathe and give the body a break from the same old positions.

Stretching won't fix everything, but it can interrupt discomfort before it sets in too deep. A small act, done often, helps us function just a little bit better.

REFRESH WITH COLD WATER

There's something wildly underrated about cold water. Whether it's a splash to the face, a cool flannel on the back of the neck, a brisk shower or dipping our toes into the sea, cold water wakes us up in the most deliciously jarring way.

Cold water is grounding and invigorating. It calms a racing mind, soothes inflammation, lifts our mood thanks to that zing of endorphins it triggers and snaps us into the present.

We don't need to overthink it. A moment under the cold tap can take the edge off the overwhelm. It's accessible, quick and science-backed. No fuss. No fanfare. Just a simple way to cut through the noise when we're flagging or fizzing.

Self-care isn't always warm and fluffy. Instead, it can be downright bracing.

PUNCH A PILLOW

There are moments when calm coping tools just don't cut it. When everything feels too much and we need a safe, physical outlet. Enter: the pillow. Find one that can take it, nothing too precious, and let yourself go at it. Punch. Shout. Squeeze. Throw it onto the bed if you need to.

This isn't about rage or drama. It's about release. Our bodies hold on to emotion, and sometimes, the only way to shift it is to move it through. Punching a pillow gives us somewhere to put the feelings that are too big to carry. It says: I acknowledge this. I'm not bottling it up.

Then comes the exhale. The drop in tension. That split second where we feel a little more in our bodies and a little less like we might explode. It's not about losing control. It's about reclaiming it. This, too, is self-care – giving strong feelings a safe way out.

SING OUT LOUD

Singing out loud is one of those feel-good things in life. It doesn't matter if we're in tune. We can belt it out in the shower, hum in the car or play carpool karaoke.

We don't have to sound good. We just have to let it out. Pick songs that feel like home or rebellion or release. Let the voice crack and let the feelings flow.

Singing simultaneously taps into something physical and emotional, connecting breath with sound, and memory with movement. It slows the breath, lifts the mood and helps shake off tension we didn't know we were carrying.

Music and voice bypass overthinking and meet us where we are. That's what makes it self-care – accessible, effective and ours. No stage required.

Self-care means giving the world the best of you instead of what is left of you.

KATIE REED

DANCE

Dancing gets us out of our heads and into our bodies in a playful and primal way. A bop in the kitchen. A shimmy while brushing our teeth. A whole-body wiggle with the curtains drawn. Let the beat find us. Let it shake something loose.

Dancing is self-care because it reminds us that joy can live in the body. That we don't need permission to feel good. That we can move through stuckness with rhythm and a bit of ridiculousness.

So we press play. We let our limbs lead. We stop worrying about what it looks like – and remember how good it feels. We laugh, move and lose ourselves for a song or two. And when the music stops, we often feel a little lighter. A little looser. A little more like ourselves again.

FLY A KITE

A kite, a little wind, and a willingness to look a little ridiculous as we seek to find the gust that'll set the kite soaring.

Flying a kite is simple, light and a little bit magical. It pulls our eyes up and out, away from screens and to-do lists. Even if it's wonky or only catches the wind for a few seconds, it's not about getting it perfect. It's about being outside, moving, looking up, laughing and letting go a little. Giddy? Maybe. But it captures something important: joy for joy's sake.

There's something freeing about holding the string in our hands and feeling it tug in the wind – like we're part of something bigger. It reminds us what fun feels like when no one's watching.

Self-care sometimes looks like us, slightly out of breath, cheeks flushed, eyes bright, chasing the wind and remembering how good it is to play.

TAPPING INTO OUR SENSES

Sensory self-care is one of the most primitive ways to change our emotional state. Our senses bring us back into our body, rooting us in the present moment. This is especially helpful during periods of anxiety, burnout, sadness or overstimulation.

Smell

Scent is fast-acting. It bypasses logic and goes straight to the emotional part of the brain. That's why one smell can instantly trigger calm, comfort or a strong memory. Try:

+ Lighting a scented candle you love.
+ Using essential oils like lavender, eucalyptus or bergamot.
+ Wearing a perfume or body lotion that comforts.
+ Sniffing fresh herbs or citrus.
+ Opening the window after it rains.
+ Treating yourself to fresh flowers.

Touch

Physical touch, texture, pressure and temperature help regulate the nervous system and create a sense of safety. When thoughts are racing, or emotions feel loud, grounding through touch can offer steady, quiet reassurance. Try:

+ Wrapping up in a warm jumper or soft blanket.
+ Running your hands under warm or cool water.
+ Holding a smooth stone, fidget toy or piece of fabric.
+ Rubbing a moisturizer into your hands slowly.
+ Using a weighted blanket or heat pack.
+ Letting your bare feet touch the earth or floor.

Sight

What we look at changes how we feel. Visual input can either overwhelm or calm us, depending on what we're taking in. A shift in our visual environment can help signal safety, order or beauty, especially in moments of inner chaos. Try:

+ Looking at a photo that makes you feel something good.
+ Watching the sky shift.
+ Creating a visual corner that feels calming to look at.
+ Noticing light and shadow around the room.
+ Tidying one surface or space.
+ Pausing to take in something beautiful, however small.

Sound

Sound shapes how we feel, often without us noticing. Some noises can leave us feeling overstimulated or on edge, while others help us slow down or shift gears. Being intentional about what we listen to and what we tune out can change how the moment feels. Try:

+ Playing music that matches or lifts your mood.

- Listening to gentle background noise like rainfall or birdsong.
- Sitting in silence, even briefly.
- Noticing and naming five sounds you can hear.
- Using noise-cancelling headphones or earplugs.
- Humming or singing quietly to yourself.

Taste

Taste is a simple way to ground ourselves. It's physical, immediate and easy to access. When we're overwhelmed, numb or disconnected, a favourite or familiar flavour can bring us back into the present moment. Try:

- Drinking a warm cup of chamomile tea.
- Sucking a mint or citrus sweet.
- Tasting something with a strong flavour like ginger, lemon or cinnamon.
- Eating a favourite snack without distractions.
- Chewing gum.
- Noticing texture, temperature and flavour as you eat.

MASSAGE

We carry a lot. In our shoulders. Our necks. Our jaws. The ache of holding everything together often settles into our bodies before we've even noticed. Massage is one way to ease that load, and we don't need to wait for someone else to do it.

A self-massage doesn't need oils or spa music, just a few minutes and a bit of care. Rub lotion into your feet slowly. Press into the base of your skull. Knead your jaw, your calves, your temples. Go where it's tight. Stay where it needs you.

Massage increases blood flow, calms the nervous system and brings us back into our bodies – away from the swirl of thoughts and into something solid. It's practical, effective and surprisingly calming. One more way we take care of ourselves when the tension builds.

How to give yourself a scalp massage

1. Sit or lie down somewhere you can relax your shoulders and neck.

2. Use the pads of your fingers and place both hands on your scalp.

3. Begin at the base of your skull and make small, firm circles.

4. Slowly move toward the crown of your head, then to the sides and temples.

5. Applying light pressure, notice where tension sits and spend longer there.

6. Slow breaths help your nervous system settle while your hands do the work.

MINDFULLY MOISTURIZE

Moisturizing is one of those everyday things we often forget or rush through. But when we slow it down, it becomes something else entirely – a practical and restorative moment of self-care.

After a shower or before bed, apply lotion or oil for a few moments. Start at your feet and work upward toward the heart. Use slow, firm strokes. Notice any dry patches, tightness or tenderness. Linger a little longer where it's needed.

This simple ritual helps boost circulation, supports the skin's barrier and offers a chance to reconnect with the body after a long day or night. It's calming, kind and gently energizing all at once. We're giving back to a body that's carried us through. Moisturizing like this reminds us that self-care is always within reach and doesn't have to be complicated.

GIVE YOURSELF PERMISSION TO BLOOM

HAVE A PAMPER SESSION

Pampering is often dismissed as indulgent or frivolous. But it's not; it's sensory self-care. It tells our bodies: you're safe. You're worth looking after. You matter. Pampering ourselves might look like painting our nails while the dinner is in the oven. Letting a warm flannel rest over tired eyes. Sitting on the edge of the bathtub with our feet in warm water and our phones out of reach.

It's brushing our hair slowly instead of yanking through tangles. Using the good body lotion because today is as good a day as any. Pulling on freshly washed pyjamas straight from the radiator. Massaging our hands with cream while the kettle boils. Slathering on lip balm as we read a book. Making a DIY face mask and lying down for 10 minutes with our eyes closed.

Pampering doesn't have to take a chunk of time or be an activity we partake in solely to look good in a photo or for a night out. Taking just 5 or 10 minutes of gentle, kind care can bring us back to our bodies.

DIY face mask

1. Mix 1 tablespoon of plain yoghurt with 1 teaspoon of honey and a teaspoon of oats.

2. Apply to clean skin, avoiding the eyes.

3. Leave on for 10–15 minutes.

4. Rinse with warm water and pat dry.

5. Follow with your usual moisturizer.

SEEK COMFORT IN CLOTHES OR A WARM BLANKET

Warm layers, soft textures and familiar clothes can signal to the nervous system that we're safe. This is about support over style.

Reach for the jumper that's worn in and warm. Pull on thick socks. Wrap up in a heavy blanket. Add a beanie, a scarf or the cardigan that's practically part of the furniture. These small sensory signals help the body regulate under stress and shift into a calmer state.

Certain fabrics, weights and fits can be naturally soothing. Loose waistbands, fleece linings, brushed cotton, the weight of a blanket across the shoulders – these offer practical relief when everything feels a bit too much.

Comfort helps us manage. It reduces sensory overwhelm, lowers stress and creates the conditions for rest or recovery. This is self-care at its most straightforward, and it really works.

EAT A NOURISHING SNACK

Low energy? Eat something. A steady, satisfying snack can change how we feel physically and emotionally. Everything feels more challenging when we haven't eaten enough, and even the most minor tasks feel like a stretch.

A proper snack can make a surprising difference: a slice of toast, a boiled egg, a bowl of soup or fruit with peanut butter.

Skipping meals or grazing on crumbs might feel normal in busy seasons, but we deserve better than running on fumes. We're not machines, but food *is* fuel, and it helps regulate our mood, supports our nervous system and gives us the energy to keep going.

Eating is everyday self-care. It is one of the most basic ways we can look after ourselves. A good snack won't fix the day, but it might make everything feel a little more manageable. And that's worth pausing for.

PUT ON FRESH BEDDING

There's something about sliding into a clean, soft bed with fresh sheets that tops the chart of life's quiet luxuries. It's bliss.

Tending to our environment is a way of tending to ourselves. Changing our bedding can be a reset when we feel flat, foggy or stagnant.

It doesn't take much, but the impact is real – like turning down the noise of the day and signalling to our body that comfort is coming. It's a relatively small task that elicits a deep, relaxing exhale at the end of a rough day – self-care in cotton form. We can add a favourite pillow spray, fluff the duvet, pop on our cosiest pyjamas and make it a ritual – not just for special occasions, but for the ordinary ones too.

PLAY WITH A PET

Animals don't care about deadlines, to-do lists or whether we've folded our laundry. They just want our time, a cuddle and to play.

Playing with a pet soothes the nervous system, quiets the mind and offers connection without pressure. It's grounding, comforting and often hilarious – all in one. We breathe more deeply. We smile without meaning to.

No pet? No problem. Borrow one from a friend, visit a rescue centre or spend a few minutes watching feel-good animal clips. It's not the same, but it still gives the brain a break and lifts the mood.

Animals don't need us to be anyone other than exactly who we are. And when we spend time with them, we're reminded that we're loveable as we are – no fixing, no filter, just us.

DO A SPOT OF GARDENING

Gardening gets us outside, gets us moving and gives us something to focus on beyond our own thoughts. It's physical enough to shift stagnant energy, gentle enough not to overwhelm, and satisfying in a way that screens and to-do lists just aren't. Pull a few weeds. Water a windowsill herb. Repot a plant.

There's a rhythm to gardening. Small beginnings, visible progress, a clear sense of completion, and the cycles of the seasons. When everything around us feels discombobulated, gardening offers structure.

It also teaches us how to care without rushing the outcome, for nature takes its time. We learn to pay attention to what thrives in certain conditions, what needs more light, and what needs cutting back. We become part of nature's cycle and there's something deeply restorative about remembering we're allowed to move through our own natural cycles and seasons, too.

We don't expect a plant to bloom without the right support – and we shouldn't expect that of ourselves either. Growth takes time.

LIE DOWN WITH YOUR LEGS UP A WALL

Lying flat with your legs raised against a wall or resting on a chair supports circulation, reduces swelling in the feet and legs, and relieves pressure on the lower back. This exercise is especially beneficial when we've been standing for long stretches or sitting in the same position all day.

It also helps calm the nervous system. Just 5–10 minutes can lower the heart rate, regulate breathing and ease the body into a more restful state. It's used in yoga and physical therapy for a reason – it's self-care that works.

This simple posture can be a powerful tool for winding down after a full day or steadying ourselves mid-stress. We don't need to do anything but lie back and let gravity take over.

TAKE A BATH

A bath can draw a line under the day. It signals a shift from doing to doing nothing, from holding it together to letting it go. Warm water helps relax tense muscles, soothe aching joints and ease the nervous system into a calmer state.

No need for a whole routine. Just run the water, get in and let it do its thing. Add Epsom salts if you have them – the magnesium can help reduce inflammation, support sleep and ease stress. Bubbles or a few drops of essential oil are optional extras.

Lower the lights or leave them as they are. Play music or enjoy the quiet. Let your jaw unclench. Let your breath slow. Let yourself stop.

There's no right way to take a bath. The benefit is in the act itself – pausing long enough to say: *I've done enough for today. Now I rest.*

BUY SOME FLOWERS

Flowers are a gentle reminder that beauty doesn't need to be useful to be valuable. You're allowed to have something lovely for the sole reason you want to and like it.

Buying flowers for yourself is a subtle, almost defiant act of self-kindness. There's something quietly life-affirming about it. Not for an occasion or as a treat. Just because. It doesn't need to be an expensive bouquet, just something which makes you smile in appreciation as you walk by; perhaps it's the colour you're drawn to, the shapes, the textures.

Pop your blooms in a jar by your bed, on your desk or next to the kettle and let them be a nod to your worth and a reminder that you don't have to earn self-care.

BREATHE IN... AND BREATHE OUT...

Our mind and body work in sync, simultaneously transferring millions of messages per second. What goes on in our mind has a strong influence on what happens to our physiology, and vice versa.

When we're feeling stressed or anxious, our mind sends signals to our body that there is a perceived threat and we need to be primed to fight, flight or freeze. Rapid breathing and a quickened heart rate are symptoms of this response, as if the danger were real, they would help us to spring into action more quickly. Oftentimes, though, the threat exists only in our thoughts, and our body doesn't know the difference between what's real and what's not.

Thankfully, just as our mind can influence our body, our body can influence our mind. Simply adjusting our breathing can signal for the body to back down, sending it information that we're now safe and to step out of its "high alert" status. Here are some tried-and-tested breathing techniques:

4-7-8 breathing

1. Inhale deeply through your nose for 4 seconds.
2. Hold your breath for 7 seconds.
3. Exhale slowly through your mouth for 8 seconds.
4. Repeat 4 to 5 times until you feel your breath start to steady.

Coherent breathing

1. Inhale for 5 to 6 seconds.
2. Exhale for 5 to 6 seconds.
3. Continue this slow, even breathing until you feel safe and calm.

Box breathing

1. Inhale through your nose for 4 seconds.
2. Hold your breath for 4 seconds.
3. Exhale through your mouth for 4 seconds.
4. Hold your breath for 4 seconds.
5. Repeat this rhythm until you feel yourself relax.

CHAPTER THREE:

MIND

The mind never really clocks off. It's at work all day remembering things, making decisions, overthinking that text we sent, juggling ideas, and trying to keep us safe. No wonder it sometimes feels tired, tangled or stuck on a loop with to-do lists piling up in the background like browser tabs we forgot to close.

When our minds are overloaded, even simple things can feel more complicated than they should. It's not about thinking happier thoughts or trying to fix ourselves. It's about slowing the spin. Lightening the load. Making room for even a little more ease.

This chapter is about making space for the kind of self-care that protects our peace and gives our minds a chance to rest, reset or refocus.

Here, we'll explore simple ways to support our mental well-being so that when life gets loud, we're not quite so swept away by it.

BE MINDFUL IN THIS MOMENT

When we're already overloaded, trying new tips and tricks can feel like the proverbial straw that broke the camel's back.

Mindfulness is amazing because it's not asking more of us, and it doesn't take extra time or need anything but *you*. It's simply about using your attention, intentionally.

Noticing the flavour, temperature and aroma of a cup of tea, soaking in the vibrancy and colours of a sunset, taking a deep, restorative breath of fresh air – these are all moments we can pause in. When we fully tune in to them, we find ourselves feeling grounded into the present.

When we start being present in the moment, those few seconds of awareness can make a huge difference and really add up. Being present is a present – a self-gift by way of a mini rest and reset: a much-needed pause.

Try this 5, 4, 3, 2, 1 mindfulness exercise

When everything feels scattered and you're struggling to remain in the present moment, this simple mindfulness exercise can help bring you back:

Take your time to pause on each step.

1. Five things you can see.
2. Four things you can feel.
3. Three things you can hear.
4. Two things you can smell.
5. One thing you can taste.

NAME WHAT YOU'RE FEELING

When your mind feels like a tangled ball of string, naming the feeling can help you find the end of the thread.

Research shows that "affect labelling" – putting emotions into words – reduces activity in the amygdala, the brain's fear centre, and increases activity in the prefrontal cortex, where rational thinking lives. In other words, naming what you feel can take away its power.

You don't need fancy language. "I'm sad", "I'm tense" or "I'm lonely" are enough. If it feels vague, try prompts like: Is this physical or emotional? What triggered it? What does it remind me of? Once you've named it, you may find it easier to respond rather than react.

Naming a feeling doesn't fix everything, but it creates space. In that space, you can make choices with kindness and clarity instead of from a place of panic and overwhelm.

WRITE OUT YOUR WORRIES

There's nothing worse than the overwhelming stress of a mind that's full of tangled mental clutter jostling for our urgent attention.

These thoughts, tasks, to-do lists, reminders and worries can pull us this way, that way, forward and backward. We don't know if we're coming or going.

A quick and helpful way to clear some mental space is to get it *all* written down. When we brain dump what's on our minds, it's like reorganizing that kitchen drawer that is too full to open properly. Decluttering by reducing the contents provides an instant reprieve.

Don't worry about how neat your writing is and whether you're spelling things correctly, just write it all down. Every ounce of it. Seeing thoughts on paper then makes it easier to organize them into what can wait, what can't and what can be set aside entirely. Some of your thoughts will be useful and will inform your next steps. Some, however, will have just been taking up space.

JOURNAL PROMPTS FOR WHEN YOU'RE STRUGGLING

Writing things down can bring a kind of relief that thinking alone rarely does. When we feel overwhelmed, muddled or stretched too thin, journalling can help us make sense of what's going on.

There's no need to write beautifully or get it "right". We're merely listening in and checking in – the basis of self-care. It doesn't need to be perfect: let it be messy and let it be honest.

These prompts are here to offer a place to start when you're not sure where to begin:

+ What's going on in my mind right now?
+ What are three things I'm carrying that feel too heavy today?
+ Is there something I need to say out loud but haven't?
+ What might I need to hear from someone I trust right now?
+ What's one thing I can let go of just for today?

- If I could call in help from anyone, what would I ask for?
- What has helped me in the past when I've felt like this?
- Who or what makes me feel safest?
- What would "enough" look like today?
- Write a short letter of compassion to yourself from a future you who's through this.
- If I could give myself permission for anything right now, what would it be?
- What might "self-care" look like for me in the next 10 minutes?

HAVE A GOOD CRY

Crying isn't a sign that we're failing to cope. It's not weakness, it's release. A way for the body to let go of the pressure that's been building under the surface.

Sometimes, we know exactly why the tears are there. Other times, they arrive unannounced without a neat explanation. That's okay. We don't need a reason. We can just let go and let them flow.

Cry in the car if you need to. Or in the bath, in bed, curled under a blanket. Cry while watching a film that resonates with exactly how you're feeling. Wherever it happens, let the emotion move through you in your own time.

Crying is one of the most honest forms of self-care. It doesn't ask us to fix anything; it just asks us to feel.

TAKE A NAP

There's something wonderfully ordinary *and* mighty about a nap. Just a short pause – a moment to stop, close our eyes and let the world fall away for a while. Even 20 minutes can help. Lie on the sofa. Pull a blanket over your shoulders. Let your eyes rest.

We're not failing if we need to stop. We're not machines, we're human. Naps aren't lazy, they're smart. And sometimes, the kindest, cleverest thing we can do is let ourselves drift off and return when we're steadier. Naps are the body saying: I need a minute. And us saying: I'm listening.

Naps help settle a frazzled nervous system. They bring calm to the chaos. And often, when we wake, we find things feel just a little bit more manageable.

SAY "NO" MORE

"No" is one of the simplest words and sentences we have and is one of the most difficult to say.

When we mean "not right now" or "I don't have the capacity", we can't quite get the words out. We say *yes* when we mean *no*. It's often easier to agree than to disappoint, but over time, all those yeses take a toll.

Saying *no* can feel uncomfortable, especially at first, but it protects our time, energy and peace of mind. It keeps us from stretching ourselves so thin that there's nothing left.

No doesn't have to be harsh. It can be quiet and clear. "That's not going to work for me." "I can't commit to that right now." "I need to pass."

Every *no* makes space for a *yes* elsewhere. A *yes* that honours what matters most, including you.

SET BOUNDARIES WITH YOUR OWN THOUGHTS

We often think of boundaries as something we set with other people, but they can be just as important internally. Not every thought deserves your full attention. Some are intrusive, unhelpful or downright cruel. Learning to recognize and redirect these thoughts is a form of self-respect (and self-respect is the highest form of self-care).

When a thought loops or drags you down, try saying – either aloud or in your head – "That's not helpful right now," or "I'm not going there today." This isn't denial; it's discernment. It's reminding yourself that you don't have to entertain every idea your mind presents.

Research into cognitive defusion supports the idea that creating space between you and your thoughts reduces their power. You are not your thoughts. Setting mental boundaries helps you decide what gets your energy and what doesn't.

INTERRUPT SPIRALLING THOUGHTS

We're an imaginative bunch, but sadly, our imagination tends to run away with itself when it comes to worst-case scenarios.

Interrupting the spiral when your mind starts replaying conversations, catastrophizing about events or racing around as it ruminates is a self-care habit which can stop those patterns in their tracks.

A slight worry can snowball: one late reply means they hate me; one bad day means I'll never be okay again. When your brain gets swept up in this, try anchoring it with facts. This isn't the same as toxic positivity – it's not "Everything will be fine," but more "What do I actually know to be true right now?"

For example: "They didn't reply" becomes "They might be busy." "I failed" becomes "One thing didn't go to plan." You can also disrupt the momentum with structured tasks:

+ Count backward slowly from 50, matching each number with a breath.
+ Count objects around you: five blue things, four textures you can feel, three sounds you can hear.
+ Tap each finger to your thumb in sequence while counting from 1 to 10, then back again.
+ Set a 1-minute timer and count how many deep breaths you can take without rushing.

These easily remembered counting exercises help re-engage the parts of the brain responsible for focus and regulation, pausing the momentum long enough to get your bearings.

You alone are enough.
You have nothing to
prove to anybody.

MAYA ANGELOU

LET GO OF PERFECT

Oh boy, the pressure to get everything right is an invisible, palpable and heavy burden we carry, often without even realizing it. We strive for perfect words, perfect actions, perfect outcomes. But nothing – or anyone – is perfect.

"Perfect" is some distant, unattainable mirage.

Life is messy. To be human is to be messy and to be making mistakes, learning from them, moving on and making some more. They're how we learn, grow, adapt and progress. Think about how clumsy our first steps were as we learned to walk. Over time, we learned from every misstep and every bump.

Self-care lies in accepting our unfinishedness, our stumbles and our wrong turns. We will sometimes say and do the wrong thing. We'll sometimes wish we'd done it differently.

When that happens (because it will, that's *normal*), give yourself grace. You're just being human.

REPLACE NEGATIVE THOUGHTS

Many of us have a relentless inner critic which is extremely detrimental to our self-esteem. We get so used to this endless stream of negativity that we aren't always consciously aware of it.

Noticing the tone of that inner self-talk means we can set about to change the habit of it. After all, that's what these thoughts typically are: habit. One that can be disrupted and broken.

Gradually, and with a lot of practice, we can replace perceived flaws, mistakes and failures with the kind of encouragement and grace we'd bestow upon a friend.

When one of those critical thoughts pops in, pause and ask yourself: What would I say to a friend in this instance? What's softer, kinder, truer?

Lead instead with that. Repeat it over and over until a newer, gentler voice is the norm.

KEEP A POSITIVITY JAR

A positivity jar is a quiet little lighthouse for the rough days, guiding us toward calmer and safer shores. It's about making sure the light doesn't get lost in the dark.

Here's how to create one:

1. Find a jar or container. It doesn't have to be anything fancy; a jam jar or shoebox will suffice.

2. Each time something good happens, write it down and pop it in the jar – a kind word, a small win, a glimmer of hope. You can use a Post-it, a scrap of paper, the back of a receipt – whatever's to hand.

3. Those scraps of paper are the evidence that good things happen and that you've weathered more than you realize. When things feel bleak, reach in. Read the proof that you are more than the sum of this bad day.

Self-care is collecting kindness on purpose – so you don't have to go looking for it when you're too tired to search.

TAKE A DIGITAL DETOX

Those smartphones of ours can affect our mental health in less than desirable ways. They're built to be used constantly, but the endless notifications and others' expectation that we're always available can leave us feeling run ragged.

How to take a digital break

1. Having an idea of what you'll do (or not do) with the additional headspace and time is helpful. As is letting people know in advance that you'll be offline.

2. Either pop your device on aeroplane mode or turn it off and set it somewhere out of reach. At first, not having our devices so readily available can feel pretty uncomfortable. We're so used to reaching for them without thinking that it's natural to feel a sense of loss and a bit fidgety. The silence, the stillness – it can feel unsettling. That's normal.

3. That restlessness or boredom? Use it. Go for a walk. Revisit a craft project. Write a letter to a friend. Bake or cook something.

4. After a while, you should notice that, without the constant noise of notifications or new posts, you feel less rushed, less responsive to external stimuli.

5. When it's time to reconnect, be intentional about any boundaries you'd like to pop in place. Do you need to re-enable every notification? Could going offline be a regular thing, like screen-free evenings after a certain time of day? The detox isn't just about taking a break; it's about reflecting on your relationship with technology so that it works for you.

CHECK YOUR MENTAL INPUT

We're all aware that the food we eat caters to our biological functions working optimally.

The same can be said for what we mentally consume. If we're overloading on negative, heavy, dark and sad content, then we'll feel negative, heavy, dark and sad.

In fact, when we do so, we're literally rewiring our brain to look for more of that sort of content. The more we expose ourselves to anything repeatedly, the more our brain creates what are known as neural pathways which, over time, make seeking for that content automatic. This can shape our perspective, influencing how we feel and how we see the world. Just like with food, balance matters – what we consume mentally can either nourish us or drain us.

Don't worry, these pathways can be diverted over time and with practice. Try limiting news checks, following social media accounts and watching TV shows which spark positivity, and reading books or listening to podcasts which uplift and inspire.

LEARN A NEW WORD OR FACT

Learning something small gives the brain a job to do – something focused, light and free from pressure. And that's often precisely what we need when our thoughts feel heavy or stuck.

Rather than take on anything particularly studious or taxing, we can follow the flicker of curiosity. We can pull on threads and fall down rabbit holes of feel-good knowledge and random facts. What does that word mean? How does bread rise? Why do cats purr?

This kind of learning activates the brain without demanding too much. It brings a sense of progress and possibility – which can be especially helpful on days that feel flat or foggy. Our mind enjoys being engaged, stretched and surprised.

DISTRACT YOURSELF

There are times when the kindest thing we can do is turn the noise down a little. Not to avoid what's going on but to catch our breath before we face it again. When everything feels tangled, and our thoughts won't let up, self-care means turning the volume down just enough to catch our breath.

Pick something that doesn't ask too much – something light, familiar and soothingly repetitive. Bake, do a puzzle while listening to a podcast, rearrange a shelf, read a book, shred that paperwork, pull up the weeds in your garden, doodle or watch an episode of your favourite TV programme.

It's about giving our brain a break from the noise. Letting our thoughts slow down. Distraction gets a bad name, but when used with care, it's a helpful tool; a bridge between overwhelm and okay.

READ A BOOK

Some kinds of rest don't look like rest at all – and reading is one of them.

Getting lost within the pages of a novel, cookbook, comic or memoir gives the brain a gentle focus. As too, can allowing an audiobook to unfold in our ears. A chance to step out of our own thoughts and into another space, even if only for a few pages.

Reading creates a pause and offers perspective, rhythm, structure and story. It gives our minds something to hold on to – something steady, absorbing and calm.

We don't have to finish a chapter or even fully concentrate. Just let the words keep us company. Let them take the edge off the day.

When we're overwhelmed, books and stories give our minds a place to rest and reset. It slows us down without switching us off. That's self-care – giving ourselves something steady to focus on, something that gently interrupts the noise.

DECLUTTER YOUR SURROUNDINGS

Our surroundings affect how we feel. Clutter can become visual noise – tiny stress signals whispering, "You should deal with this," every time we walk by.

Clutter doesn't build overnight; it builds gradually: paperwork we'll "get to later", drawers that no longer close and piles of clothes on the floor.

Decluttering is about creating pockets of peace. The goal isn't perfection: it's relief and ease. Self-care is making your space feel like it works *for* you, not against you.

We don't need to tackle an entire room in one go. Small shifts such as clearing that drawer, donating one bag of unworn clothes, and tidying and wiping one kitchen surface can bring some much-welcomed mental breathing room. Try decluttering:

+ Expired medication, makeup or toiletries.
+ Mugs, socks or Tupperware missing their partners.
+ That one drawer of "everything" that stresses you out.
+ Clothes that no longer fit who you are.
+ Screenshots, tabs or unused apps on your phone.
+ Subscriptions you forgot you had.
+ The pile of unopened post.
+ Books you're never going to read.
+ Social media follows that make you feel "less than".
+ To-do lists with things you no longer want to do.

**SAY "YES"
TO ALL THAT
LIGHTS YOU UP**

GAZE AT THE CLOUDS

Find the sky. Any bit will do. Through a window, over a fence, between two buildings – it all counts. Let your eyes relax and follow the clouds for a while. You don't have to name the shapes you can see – though you absolutely can if you want to.

We're often stuck in our heads, hunched over our to-do lists, phones and computers. Looking up instead of down gives us a different perspective – one that feels just a little more spacious.

Clouds don't rush; they drift. They move at their own pace and remind us that everything shifts – even thoughts, even feelings.

Cloud-gazing is self-care that asks very little. Just our attention, a brief pause and the willingness to stop for a moment. It's a way to reset, a way to come back to ourselves without doing anything much at all.

THE 1-MINUTE BREATH ANCHOR

There are times when our mood starts to spin on a downward spiral, and we feel a little helpless to stop it. The 1-minute breath anchor is a self-care tool for this exact moment when stress and anxiety threaten to overwhelm us.

1. Turn your attention to your breath and notice the in and the out, the rise and the fall.

2. Place a hand on your chest or stomach and feel it move with each inhale and exhale.

3. Your thoughts will wander, and when they do, gently bring your attention back to your breath.

4. Keep going until you feel anchored back into the moment, spiral averted.

TRY A NEW HOBBY

Trying something new wakes the brain, shakes off the cobwebs and makes room for play. It doesn't matter if we're any good to begin with – what matters is that our interest is piqued, and our curiosity has somewhere to go.

Learning how to play a musical instrument, signing up for a cooking class, watching YouTube tutorials on how to knit, or finally giving watercolours a go… Pick something that makes you smile or think, *I've always wanted to try that.*

Let it be just for you – no pressure, no performance. New hobbies give us space to explore and expand. They invite play back in. Some things can exist simply because they're joyful.

Self-care is allowing ourselves to try, play and learn without needing to master. It's allowing ourselves to enjoy something purely because it feels good in the moment – and that's a good enough reason to begin.

MAKE THAT DOCTOR APPOINTMENT

It's easy to put off the appointments. The form-filling. The phone calls. We tell ourselves it's probably nothing or that we'll sort it out next week. We wait (and worry) and wait some more.

Self-care is sometimes the most grown-up thing we do – picking up the phone, booking the appointment, asking for support.

That mole we've been meaning to get checked? The brain fog we keep brushing off? The overdue eye test we're embarrassed about? The symptoms we've googled ten times? We don't have to go alone. We can take someone with us. We can ask for help. We *matter*.

Make the appointment. It's not wasting anyone's time, and you're not taking resources from someone you deem more "deserving". *You* deserve more than just to get by – *you* deserve to be well and for your mind to be put to rest.

DO SOMETHING THAT MAKES YOU FEEL CAPABLE

Sometimes, we face an obstacle or challenge that looms too big to handle, leaving us feeling helpless and hopeless.

Doing something we're good at, no matter how small, reminds our brain that we're not helpless or hopeless. It could be organizing a drawer, fixing a leaky tap, helping someone with a problem, making a perfect cup of tea or answering a quiz question correctly.

Capable doesn't need to mean "productive" or "impressive"; just something that makes us feel competent and can-do. Giving our mind evidence that we *can* do things can shift our self-talk from "I can't cope" to "Maybe I can." That tiny nudge helps reset our mental landscape, especially when anxiety or low mood narrows our perspective.

Even when nothing else feels certain, remembering our resourcefulness is a quiet, enduring self-care.

CREATE A BEDTIME ROUTINE

Our minds don't always know when to switch off. That's where routines can help – not as strict rules, but as familiar signals that guide us from doing into resting.

A bedtime routine doesn't need to be elaborate or time-consuming. Just a few small cues that tell your brain: the day is done. Dim the lights. Put your phone on charge. Stretch, journal, read, breathe. Let the pace shift. Let the noise settle.

Repeating the same steps most nights helps the mind recognize what comes next. Over time, that pattern becomes a kind of shorthand – a way to say: we've done enough now.

Not another thing to tick off, but a gentle bridge between busy and calm. A chance to ease into rest instead of crashing into it. Ideas to try:

+ Switch to warmer lighting an hour before bed.
+ Put your phone on charge and out of reach.
+ Brew a herbal tea or a mug of warm milk and take your time drinking it.

- + Keep a notebook by the bed for a quick brain dump – anything that's swirling or won't leave you alone.
- + Read something easy and comforting.
- + Stretch.
- + Wash your face or apply some lotion with care, not rush.
- + You could play gentle music, white noise or nature sounds.
- + Light a candle.
- + Tidy one small corner of the room to create a sense of calm.

Self-care for the mind often begins here – in the small choices that help us step out of the day and into rest.

MAKE A VISION BOARD

A vision board is a way of tuning into ourselves and capturing our hopes, desires and feelings of the life we want to move toward. It is not a checklist or a five-year plan – just a collection of images, words and colours that feel like *you*.

It's about paying attention to what lights us up and placing that happiness, interest and possibility somewhere we can see it.

Our vision board might be taped to the bathroom mirror. It might be on the inside of a wardrobe door or tucked inside a notebook only we ever see. Maybe it's a collage, or perhaps it's digital. Whatever shape it takes, it's a personal and creative reminder of what matters. Tips for creating your own:

+ Use old magazines, postcards, photos, Pinterest printouts.

- Don't overthink – if it sparks something, it belongs.
- Include colours, textures and feelings – not just goals.
- Add your word of the year, a favourite quote or a phrase that lifts you.
- Focus on how you want to *feel*, not just what you want to do.
- Let it grow and change – it's allowed to evolve with you.
- Keep it somewhere visible or tucked away for quiet reminders.

A vision board is a self-care tool – a visual reminder of what energizes us. It helps us stay connected to our values, joy and sense of direction.

CHAPTER FOUR:

SPIRIT

There's a part of us that isn't mind or body – it's the inner-being part that lights up when we feel connected or quietly content. The part that feels the most like us when everything else falls away. That's our spirit, and it needs care, too.

Spiritual self-care is about tuning into what gives life meaning – the things that quietly nourish us. It might be time in nature, making something with our hands, laughing with people who get us, or simply feeling calm after a long stretch of not.

In this chapter, we'll tend to that inner spark – the part that's easy to lose in the noise but always worth returning to. Self-care for the spirit is about reconnecting with what matters, returning to ourselves and feeling firmly rooted in who we are.

SPEND TIME IN NATURE

Nature is a steadfast and nurturing self-care tool that doesn't ask for anything from us. If we show up in nature feeling frazzled, distracted, irritated or tired, nature will simply meet us there and gently bring us back to ourselves.

Spending time outside, even for a few minutes, can restore and rejuvenate. Five minutes noticing the sky, sitting on a bench with the sun on our face and feeling the breeze on our skin, listening to birdsong, watching the sea ebb and flow, trailing our hands through long grass or dipping our bare feet into a stream are some of the ways nature can soothe away stress and boost our mood.

Self-care really can be as simple as letting nature in, allowing it to remind us of our softness, our strength and our interconnectedness with all else.

TRY TREE BATHING

Tree bathing, or *shinrin-yoku*, began in Japan in the 1980s as a response to rising stress and burnout.

Spending time among trees and allowing yourself to "be" gives nature a chance to do its work. Research shows that even a short visit to a woodland or park can lower blood pressure, reduce cortisol and improve mood.

Engage your senses. Breathe in the scent of the forest. Watch the movement of branches as the breeze filters through them. Listen out for birdsong, the creaking of tree limbs and the rustle of leaves. Feel the different textures. Taste the fresh air as you inhale and exhale.

You don't need a forest. A few trees in a park will do. What matters is being present. Tree bathing helps calm the body, clear the mind and reconnect us to something bigger than ourselves.

WATCH A SUNSET OR SUNRISE

When we pay attention to the sky, we realize it's ever-evolving. No two seconds are the same. The clouds drift in their differing shapes, hues and sizes. The sky can be the brightest of blues or the most ominous of greys.

Watching a sunset or sunrise is a comforting act of self-care that reminds us that, while all around us may feel chaotic, some things remain certain and steady – the sun will always rise again. Whether you choose to head to the coast, sit quietly by a window in your dressing gown or wrap up on a garden seat with a cosy blanket, there's something breathtakingly awe-inspiring in seeing the gentle beginning or slow end of the day as the sky transforms into a canvas of pinks, peaches and lilacs.

SPEND TIME NEAR WATER

There's a reason we often find ourselves drawn to water. Studies show that being near it can lower cortisol, reduce anxiety and ease overstimulation. It activates the parasympathetic nervous system, which helps the body shift from stress into a more relaxed state.

Find a way to be near it. Walk beside a stream. Sit quietly by a pond. Swim in a lake (if it's safe to do so), watch the rain patter on the window or paddle in the sea if you can. However we do it, water gives the senses something to hold on to. Its movement is rhythmic. Its presence is sound, steady and calming without asking anything of us.

Spending time near water also reminds us of things we quickly forget: that life moves in cycles, that we're allowed to ebb and flow, and that force isn't always necessary – soft persistence has power, too.

FIND SOMETHING WITH HISTORY

There are things around us that have survived through the ages. Think cathedrals, castles, old trees, rocks, ruins and even antique objects. These things carry the marks of time. They've been exposed to the elements, handled by generations and are *still here*.

In a fast-paced world, being around what's lasted offers a kind of steadying. It takes us out of our stress or overwhelm and connects us to a bigger timeline. We remember we're part of something larger that didn't begin or end with today's to-do list.

This is self-care that grounds us by placing things in context. Find something with history. Visit a museum. Sit beneath the old oak in the park. Run your hand along a stone wall. Hold a family heirloom. Notice the wear, the cracks, the craftsmanship. Consider what it's been through, *endured* through. Consider what you've been through and overcome.

RETURN TO A PLACE THAT SHAPED YOU

Most of us have memories of places which make us smile when we recall them. Perhaps that's our childhood home, the spot we had our first kiss, a café we used to visit with friends and family, or the seaside town we would return to year after year. These memories are more than nostalgic; they're woven with our stories and the different iterations of who we are and who we've been.

Revisiting them – either by going back in person or simply by taking a trip down memory lane – can bring up a mix of emotions. It gives us a moment to notice what's changed, what we've kept and how far we've come. Revisiting the past in this way (with care) also helps anchor the past with the present, reconnecting us to our own timeline.

USE VISUALIZATION TO ESCAPE TO AN INNER CALM SPACE

Sometimes, the world feels too much, and we feel bulldozed flat by it. When that happens, it can help us to visit somewhere calm inside our minds. This is called visualization, and it's about using our imagination to make space and provide ourselves with a moment of steadiness when we need a self-care pause button.

1. Sit or lie somewhere comfortable.
2. Close your eyes and picture a place that feels calm, soothing and safe. This place could be real, like your cosy bed or warm bath, or it could be imagined, like a cosy cabin in the forest.
3. Take your time imagining the details. What can you see? Hear? Smell? Feel beneath your feet or around you? Let yourself settle into the calm of that place. This is your little sanctuary.
4. You can visit any time you need to feel grounded or held.

NOTICE THE SMALL JOYS

When we're feeling frazzled, finding joy can feel like a lot of effort, as though it's out of reach. The thing about joy is that we often look at it as being some boisterous firework explosion of energy, fun and light.

Joy does not always arrive so exuberantly. More often, joy is found in the reprieves – the first sip of a favourite warm drink or a nose-nudge from a furry friend. We can proactively chase these small joys and build them into our days and ways. Perhaps we can press pause for a moment to drink that delicious drink as we sit outside and enjoy the sound of birdsong.

Maybe we can treat ourselves to a bunch of tulips to brighten a windowsill for the week to come.

Big joy is awesome, but these small (often underestimated) joys can totally change the trajectory of a day, too.

MEDITATE

Meditation gives us space to be with ourselves exactly as we are. Meditating offers a reprieve, a recalibration, a moment out of the hustle and bustle of life.

We can sometimes get wrapped up in wanting to meditate "perfectly", but there's actually no such thing. There's no wrong or right way to do it. You don't have to sit still, cross-legged on the floor, or have some fancy pillow or incense sticks burning (although there's nothing wrong with those choices, either – *your* way is the best way). Meditation can be as basic as simply noticing the breath, slowing down and tuning into yourself.

During meditation, it's normal for our thoughts to wander. When we notice that and then bring our attention back to the present moment over and over again, that right there is the essence of it all.

TRY THIS LOVING-KINDNESS MEDITATION

Consider this meditation part of your self-care toolkit for use when you're being hard on yourself. It reminds us that kindness begins inside and that we're deserving of the same love and care we so often give to others.

1. Sit quietly and repeat these phrases gently, aloud or in your head: May I be calm. May I be peaceful. May I be kind. May I feel loved.

2. You can keep these wishes just for yourself or begin to extend them to others. Begin with someone you love, move on to someone you feel neutral toward, and then someone who challenges you (if that feels okay).

3. Finally, extend those same wishes to everyone everywhere.

CREATE SOMETHING, JUST BECAUSE

We often create with a goal in mind, whether to sell, gift or post on social media. But there's a different kind of self-care and value in creating something for no reason, just because…

Creative self-expression can calm the nervous system, ease anxiety and help us process thoughts and emotions in ways that words can't always reach.

This doesn't have to be complicated or time consuming. You might doodle on the back of an envelope, shape something from clay, write a haiku or bake a loaf of bread. Try folding an origami shape, making a collage or stringing a few beads onto thread.

Engaging the creative part of the brain gives the problem-solving parts a break. When we create just for the sake of it, we give ourselves space to explore without expectation, reconnecting us with curiosity, playfulness and a sense of possibility. The act of making is the self-care.

MAKE OR BAKE

Self-care isn't always about slowing down – it can be about getting focused, using our hands and creating something from nothing.

Getting busy with our hands often helps to quieten our brains and gives us a sense of accomplishment and pride when we step back and say, "I made that."

When we're willing to try, be learners and forgo the desire for perfection, we find joy in each step of the process. Baking, painting, crocheting, drawing, candle making, Lego, sculpting with clay, writing, sewing, miniature modelling – whatever it is, the process of creating something with our hands can be fulfilling, meditative and grounding. There's also something satisfying about the loop of having a beginning, a middle and an end in a world where everything is constantly open and on.

RETURN TO A CHILDHOOD JOY

There's something magical about returning to something we loved as a child and reconnecting with a version of ourselves who knew how to play. Who wasn't laden with responsibilities, worries and stress. Who did things *just* because they were fun and because they wanted to.

Maybe for you, it was all about painting, jumping waves, climbing trees, skipping, colouring, collecting things, making daisy chains and watching old cartoons. It doesn't need to be impressive or "cool". In fact, the sillier, the better. This is self-care through nostalgia, play and delight. It's about giving ourselves permission to do something for no other reason than we used to love it. Sometimes, we outgrow activities. But sometimes we don't – we just forget how much joy they brought us. Try it. Let it be messy, lopsided, a bit ridiculous, but most of all, playful!

PLAY

We know play is important, which is why we prioritize "play time" for our children. Yet, there's a tipping point in life where play gets pushed aside and replaced with all manner of adulting things. This is sad because no matter our age, play remains an important part of self-care, *especially* when life feels heavy. Play is a powerful antidote to stress; it lets the light in and fosters resilience, creativity and happiness.

When we've forgotten how it feels to laugh or be silly, then play could help us to unlock that joy again. Play might look like building a sofa fort, having a water or snowball fight, dancing like a dork, singing karaoke, playing board games with friends, jumping on a trampoline, visiting an amusement park, jumping in muddy puddles, playing tag, rolling down a grassy hill or telling really silly jokes.

LAUGH OUT LOUD

A good belly laugh that has us snorting like a hyena is *the* best way to relieve tension. It also creates a memory we can feast on for years to come.

However, laughter can feel entirely out of reach when life is challenging. The funny thing about laughter is that our brains don't know the difference between a sincere bout of giggles and a fake chuckle – it'll release feel-good chemicals, regardless.

Self-care can be silly, loud and ridiculous, so rewatch that hilarious video, spend time with the person who has you in stitches without even trying, and put on that comedy series that has you snickering away.

Laughter reminds us that we're capable of joy even in the middle of a mess. Nothing is black and white; it is possible for joy and sorrow to coexist. For, it's true, laughter *really* is the best medicine.

CALL YOUR FAVOURITE PERSON

There are people in our lives who feel like balms to our souls. They're the people who love us unconditionally, who can change the tone of the day with their words and who you can be yourself with, warts and all.

When we're overwhelmed, low or stuck in our heads, reaching out can feel like climbing a mountain. It's often easier to send a quick text (and sometimes that's all we have the energy for) but there's a particular kind of comfort that comes from hearing a loved one's voice. Calling someone – just to say hello, or to cry, or to say nothing much – can change the day's trajectory. A quick call. A long ramble. A little voice note. However it looks, this is self-care through connection.

We don't need to pretend we're okay. We don't need to be chatty or cheerful or full of news. Just being on the other end of the line is enough. A reminder that we're not meant to do this alone.

The most powerful relationship you will ever have is the relationship with yourself.

STEVE MARABOLI

MAKE A PLAYLIST

Music has a way of transcending time and taking us back to a memory, a person or a place in an instant. It can also shift our mood, make us smile, evoke emotions and even boost our confidence.

Making an uplifting playlist is a powerful way to care for ourselves – it's like an immediate jolt of joy or dash of hope when we need it most. Think of the songs that feel like sunlight, the ones that remind you of that kitchen disco, the ones you sang into your hairbrush instead of a microphone. These songs spark a shimmer and a shimmy. Compile all of those into a playlist and keep it close.

You might find that you'll create different playlists for different needs, such as a compilation of power ballads for when you need a good cry, some rock anthems for those angsty, angry times, or just pure cheesy classics for times you need a pick-me-up. However we use it, music has a way of meeting us right where we are and carrying us somewhere better.

WRITE A LETTER TO SOMEONE YOU ADMIRE

Writing a letter to someone you admire directs your attention toward the qualities you value most, such as courage, kindness and integrity. Even if you never send it, the process helps you reconnect with what's important to you.

Putting thoughts into words helps organize the mind and gives a sense of structure when things feel scattered. It's reflective and grounding and can lift the mood by reminding us of the good that exists in others and in ourselves.

Who has shaped how we think? Who has helped us keep going, even from afar? A writer, a friend, a public figure, a teacher? By identifying who and what we admire, we also recognize what we value. This reflection can act as a compass, especially when feeling lost or disconnected. Quiet realignment is potent self-care.

ACCEPT HELP

In the same way you'd gladly dive in and help someone in need, others will gladly do the same for you.

Yet, there's a paradox at play whereby the times when we really need help are usually the times we feel so unworthy of it. This makes accepting help a struggle. We tell ourselves we should be able to manage. We don't want to be a burden. We worry that we're asking for too much. But self-care isn't about doing it all alone – it's about recognizing when we need support and allowing it in. No matter what, we're all worthy and deserving of support, care and kindness. Yes, that means *you*, too.

Let people show up for you, whether that's a friend who wants to drop off some freezer meals, someone listening to our unfiltered brain dump, or professional support like a doctor, therapist or helpline.

DO A GOOD DEED

Doing something kind for someone else might not sound like *self*-care, but it is. It gently nudges us out of our heads and reminds us that we're part of something bigger. Our attention shifts to the world around us and the part we can play in it.

A good deed doesn't have to be grand, expensive or for social media. Tiny acts of kindness ripple outward, but they ripple inward, too. Good deeds remind us that even when life feels difficult, even when we're feeling low or unsure of ourselves, we still have something of value to give. And importantly, we can still have a positive impact on the lives of others. Your good deed could be:

- Sending a kind text to someone or writing them a letter.
- Creating a care package for someone who is going through it.
- Sending someone flowers.
- Donating to a local food bank or school.
- Accompanying a loved one to an appointment.
- Writing a thank you note.
- Paying forward a coffee.
- Babysitting, dog-sitting or offering a lift.
- Supporting or volunteering with a charity or cause that means something to you.

WRITE YOURSELF A LETTER

We're often stellar at dishing out the wisest words and the most astute advice. Sometimes, the most rousing and kindest words are the ones we *could* offer ourselves.

Writing a letter to yourself might sound (and feel!) strange, but it's a gentle way to meet ourselves where we are with honesty, compassion and grace. The intention and outcome of writing to yourself is completely different from writing to someone else – it meets a different emotional need and offers an alternative self-care pathway.

You can write the letter from the future you to now-you, from now-you to a younger you or from the perspective of someone who cares greatly about you. Reassure, encourage, guide.

This is self-care that says: I'm listening. I'm here. And I'm doing my best to understand myself better. Tuck the letter away and read it when you need reminding of your wisdom and clarity. There's no voice quite like your own when it learns to speak tenderly.

YOU DESERVE TO BE NOURISHED, NURTURED AND SUPPORTED

BE YOUR OWN BEST FRIEND

We'd be outraged if someone spoke to us the way we too often talk to ourselves, with harsh criticism, sneering judgement and bitter impatience. In fact, we'd likely avoid them at all costs!

Of all the habits to nurture, being our own best friend is the most transformative means of self-care. Imagine how our lives would shift if we gave ourselves grace, caught the cruel thoughts and reworded them to be gentler, acknowledged our limits with zero shame, and stopped beating ourselves up for mistakes we made but learned from. Imagine how we'd bloom if we treated ourselves like a dear, beloved friend – someone whose quirks we accept, whose flaws we forgive, whose needs we respect. Imagine how we might hold ourselves taller and how high we'd hold our heads. Just imagine!

BELIEVE IN YOURSELF

We were all born with this innate and unwavering belief in ourselves. However, through life's trials and tribulations, our self-belief can take a knock, impacting how we show up in the world.

Believing in ourselves is a foundational way to self-care because it alters what we choose to do or not do, be or not be. It doesn't mean being confident all the time or having it all figured out. It means choosing to back yourself, even when your hands are shaking with nerves.

No matter what we've been through, we're undoubtedly someone worthy of rooting for. That means trusting that we're allowed to take up space, that our voice matters and that we deserve all that's great and glorious. Believe that you've got it within you to overcome anything in your way, just as you have so many times before.

ASK FOR A HUG

If actions speak louder than words, then a hug speaks volumes. It says: I see you, I've got you, rest here, you're safe. It can steady a racing mind, soften a heavy heart, and remind us – without uttering a word – that we're not alone.

Sometimes, self-care is a pause and a comforting pair of arms (or paws...). We're never too old, too strong, or too independent to need a hug.

If there's no one nearby, a self-hug works too. Wrap your arms around yourself, apply a little pressure and sway gently. It might feel awkward at first, but your body doesn't think so. It feels the shift and registers the care.

This simple act says: I am here. I'm holding myself through this. And that, too, is self-care.

WRITE A GRATITUDE LIST

Gratitude is a way to remind ourselves what still feels kind, comforting or nourishing, *even* when life is hard. Often, things we might otherwise miss because no matter how heavy it all feels, there are glimmers of light to be found even in the darkest of times.

When life feels hard, gratitude might be the last thing on our minds. But that's when it can make the most difference to our perspective. Self-care isn't about pretending everything's hunky dory when that's not our reality. Gratitude doesn't remove our struggle; instead, it points out what's *still* good.

Yes, sometimes we might need to dig deep for the gold, like the warm drink we had or the fact we're grateful for our bed. But writing a list, however small, can help us to remember that it's not all downright awful. Try for three things: slippers without holes, the kind email you received, and the unwavering love your dog showers you with each day.

PRACTISE SAYING AFFIRMATIONS

Affirmations are short, intentional phrases we say to ourselves – aloud, in writing or quietly in our minds. They help interrupt unhelpful thought patterns and give us something more nurturing to hold on to. When repeated often, they can gently shift how we see ourselves and what we believe is possible.

They're not about pretending everything's perfect, but they do plant tiny seeds of self-trust, self-worth and self-compassion. Over time, those seeds grow.

Even if we don't fully believe the words at first, that's okay. Repetition helps. Like learning any new skill, the more you practise, the more natural they feel.

Choose one or two affirmations that feel supportive, and say them slowly, like you mean them. Say them often.

They might seem small, but affirmations are powerful. They're like mini anchors – holding us steady and gently guiding us back to ourselves. Some affirmations to try:

- I am a powerhouse of confidence.
- I love myself, wholly.
- I am allowed to take up space, and take up space I will.
- There's nothing I can't overcome.
- I can and will get through this.
- I am deserving of kindness and respect.
- My needs and wants are important.
- I am a vibrant source of warmth and light.
- I am enough, as I am, in the here and now.

MAKE A SELF-CARE BOX

Sometimes, we forget what helps us feel better, especially when we're in the thick of it. A self-care box is a gentle way of gathering what soothes and supports us, ready for the moments when we need a little help remembering. It's like packing a kindness kit for your future self. The box can live by your bed, on a shelf, in a drawer – anywhere you can reach when life feels too much.

What's inside the box doesn't need to be fancy; it just needs to feel like you. And be comforting, soothing and nourishing. Full of soft reminders that you're cared for, even by you. *Especially* by you. Creating one is an act of self-kindness. Reaching for it is one, too.

What to include in your self-care box:

+ A small notebook and pen.
+ A list of things that usually help.
+ A favourite snack or herbal tea.
+ Soft socks or a blanket.
+ A comforting scent (essential oil, pillow spray, tiny candle).
+ A photo that makes you smile.
+ Meaningful cards or notes you've received from friends.
+ A fidget toy or something to squish.
+ A printed quote or affirmation.
+ A tiny craft or colouring page.
+ Anything that feels like a hug in a box.

CONCLUSION

Throughout this book, we've explored what it means to care for ourselves in the thick of life. Not the pristine, filtered, beige and edited version presented across social media, but the honest, messy, magical, non-linear, topsy-turvy rollercoaster that real life actually is.

By now, we've gathered tools for the harder days and the steadier ones, too. Some ideas will resonate, while others might take root later, and there will be ones that just aren't quite for us.

And that's okay, because this isn't a book to be ticked off. We don't have to do it all. This book is something we can return to time and time again; a place to visit when everything feels like too much or when we're looking for inspiration.

Self-care, in its truest form, helps us keep going when we feel like we're falling apart or falling back together again. It can be quiet, scrappy, practical and small. And it can also be transformative, life-changing and revolutionary.

We don't have to wait for life to calm down, for everything to fall into place or to become someone else to partake in self-care. We're always worthy of that love and care, no matter what.

There is no single way to do self-care. No perfect routine. No universal list. What matters is that we notice what's happening within and around us, stay connected to what we need, and respond with something helpful. And with care. A bucket load of self-care.

You've so *totally* got this.

RESOURCES

Websites

Balance: personalized meditation and sleep support. www.balanceapp.com

Breathwrk: breathing practices for nervous system support. www.breathwrk.com

Calm: meditations, sleep stories, breathing exercises and mindfulness. www.calm.com

Daylio: visual mood tracking and journalling. www.daylio.net

Headspace: guided meditations and focus tools for everyday care. www.headspace.com

InsightTimer: free access to thousands of meditations, music and talks. www.insighttimer.com

Reflectly: a mood-focused journalling app. www.reflectly.app

Podcasts

The Calm Christmas Podcast: slowness, meaning and seasonal care.

Happy Place: life, loss and everything in between.

How to Fail: resilience, grace and being human.

The Pause: burnout, rest and recovery.

Poetry Unbound: poetry, stillness and reflection.

Self Care Club: honest, humorous and insightful discussions.

Therapy Chat: emotionally validating and quietly grounding.

Unlocking Us: vulnerability, compassion and being human.

INDEX

A
Affirmations 148, 150
Anchor 110, 125
Anxiety 62, 110, 113, 123, 130

B
Barefoot 21, 52
Behavioural signs 19
Boundaries 12, 21, 29, 93, 100
Breathe 37, 52, 55, 75, 80, 114
Burnout 13, 33, 62, 121, 154

C
Calm 21, 36, 42, 51, 52, 54, 57, 62, 64, 77, 80, 91, 105, 114, 119, 121, 126, 129, 130, 152, 154
Comfort 14, 21, 38, 39, 47, 62, 72, 74, 135
Comparison 17
Connection 14, 21, 75, 135
Creativity 133, 138

E
Emotional signs 19
Emotional 15, 30, 48, 62, 86, 125, 130, 137
Energy 8, 16, 26, 29, 30, 37, 50, 73, 76, 92, 93, 127, 135

F
Feelings 13, 41, 47, 57, 58, 109, 116

G
Gardening 76
Gratitude, grateful 147
Grieving 38
Grounding 12, 52, 56, 63, 75, 131, 138, 154

H
Headache 31, 50

J
Journal, journalling 14, 30, 88, 154
Joy, joyful 111, 127, 131, 132, 134

L
Laughter 134
Letter 88, 100, 138, 140, 142

M
Massage 66, 67
Meditate, meditation, meditative 128
Mental health 4, 37, 100
Mental signs 19
Mindfulness 68, 84

Mistakes 97, 98, 144

Mood 8, 50, 56, 58, 64, 73, 75, 110, 113, 120, 121, 137, 138, 154

N

Nature 15, 49, 76, 115, 119, 120, 121

Negative thoughts 98

Nervous system 34, 51, 52, 63, 66, 67, 72, 73, 75, 77, 78, 91, 123, 130, 154

Noise 28, 34, 36, 41, 48, 51, 56, 64, 74, 100, 104, 105, 106, 114, 119

O

Overstimulated 34, 51, 64

Overwhelmed 65, 88, 105, 135

P

Pain 39

Perfectionism 16, 20, 25, 31, 55, 61, 88, 97, 113, 148, 152

Permission 28, 39, 44, 48, 60, 69, 88, 132

Pet 75

Phone 34, 100, 106, 112, 114

Physical signs 18

Play 61, 75, 111, 132, 133

Present moment mindfulness 62, 65, 85, 128

R

Regulate 51, 63, 72, 73, 77

Release 14, 43, 54, 57, 58, 90, 134

Reset 74, 83, 84, 105, 109, 113

Rest 14, 25, 28, 30, 35, 36, 38, 40, 44, 48, 70, 72, 78, 83, 84, 91, 105, 112, 114, 146, 154

Restore 120

Routine 40, 78, 114, 152

S

Self-respect 13, 93

Sensory 34, 48, 62, 72

Sleep 13, 14, 18, 21, 26, 28, 51, 78, 154

Smartphones 100

Social media 20, 107, 130, 140, 152

Spiralling thoughts 94

Spoon Theory 26

Stress 12, 20, 51, 52, 54, 72, 77, 78, 87, 106, 110, 120, 121, 123, 124, 132, 133

Support 32

T

Tension 43, 47, 51, 54, 55, 57, 58, 66, 67, 134

U

Uplifting 102, 137

V

Visualization, visualize 126

W

Walk, walking 8, 21, 22, 48, 51, 97, 101

Worth 8, 13, 70, 73, 79, 119, 148

Worthy 6, 13, 25, 39, 139, 145, 152

Write, writing 8, 87, 88, 99, 130, 138, 142

ANXIETY FIRST-AID KIT

Tips and Techniques to Help You Manage Anxiety in Any Situation

Claire Chamberlain

ISBN: 978-1-83799-753-4 (Hardback)

This compact go-to guide is here to provide you with advice on managing and coping with anxiety in a range of different situations

Whether you're anxious about your relationships with others, your appearance, climate change, taking exams or anything else, this book is here to help. The tips and techniques inside will allow you to better understand and manage your worries, so that you can live life to the fullest and look forward to every day with confidence!

SELF-CARE FOR EVERY DAY

Simple Tips and Soothing Quotes to Help You Feel Your Best

ISBN: 978-1-80007-674-7 (Hardback)

This beautiful book is filled with simple self-care tips and ideas to help you nurture your well-being every day

We all need to take time out every now and again to recharge our batteries. Discover the restorative power of self-care in *Self-Care for Every Day*. Within these pages you will find simple but effective tips to nourish your mind, body and soul, advice on fitting self-care into a busy schedule, and a raft of soothing quotes.

Have you enjoyed this book?
If so, why not write a review on your favourite website?

If you're interested in finding out more about our books, find us on Facebook at **Summersdale Publishers**, on Twitter/X at **@Summersdale** and on Instagram, TikTok and Bluesky at **@summersdalebooks** and get in touch. We'd love to hear from you!

Thanks very much for buying
this Summersdale book.

www.summersdale.com